AF480694

See and Believe

Inclusion and Vivid Transformation
for Individuals and Companies

BEV JENNINGS

Table of Contents

Acknowledgments

DREAMS DO COME true! It brings me joy to talk about and to be on the journey to see everyone elevate. To be able to invite you into this reflective and transformative season warms my heart. My intention is that through *See and Believe*, you will find valuable insights for your business, success self-help, inclusive leadership and more.

My nephew, Conrad Jennings, shared this quote with me by Helen Keller: "Alone we can do so little, together we can do so much." This book exemplifies the action of togetherness because several people have shined light into SEE Company, the SEE brand and the culmination of *See and Believe*.

First, I thank my Heavenly Father, who makes all things possible. Together we elevate. Thank you to my parents Emma and Leo Jennings, grandparents John Ely and Acenia Jennings and Lonnie and Annie Koonce, siblings Larry, Debra and Drexie, and an inseparable extended family unit of uncles, aunts, and cousins. I was raised by a village including the Mt. Tabor Missionary Baptist Church, Greenwood Chapel Church and the Greenwood community. I was blessed to have a wonderful home life. Thank you for being the foundation on which I stand. Our roots of Greenwood, Florida extend for the world to see!

Thank you to my Johnson & Johnson former colleagues, like family. You and our credo will forever be etched in my heart.

Thank you to our SEE Company clients, customers, employees, suppliers, and advocacy groups. We are better, and our value is greater, because of you.

The "Light Lessons" section in *See and Believe* showcases remarkable people who have been on the SEE journey with me. Thank you for sharing your talent, knowledge, and wisdom: Doris Dickens (Family), Ericka Dunlap (Ambassador), Terri Hall (Marketing), Patricia Hill (Trends), Necole Neal (Executive) and David Ogunrinde (Branding). And thank you to LVMH's Greg Morley and Human First Advocate Paul E. Wolfe for sharing your DEI acumen and perspectives.

My decision and movement to write *See and Believe* led me on a year-long search for the right collaborator. And yes, the company name piqued my interest! Thank you, Candi Cross of You Talk I Write, creative extraordinaire, for thoughtfully engaging, immersing in the ecosystem of diversity and inclusion, and helping to bring my first book to life—and light through your expertise. Teamwork does make the dream work!

In the years ahead, I hope this book will serve as a forever companion as you transform your world to see and believe, to see everyone elevate.

Vision of a World Transformed

> *"The really wonderful thing that happened to me when I was in space was this feeling of belonging to the entire universe."*
>
> —MAE JEMISON, ASTRONAUT

WANDERING THROUGH A wonderland of beauty such as Claude Monet's Garden in Giverny, you can almost feel the color seep into your eyes and drip onto the thousands of flowers. Skin tingling, hair on your head standing. Pure awe. What a human sensation. Experiences like this enrich my soul and lift my spirit in so many ways. What's inspiring about the artist behind these orchestrations of colors and shapes beyond the obvious—extraordinary talent—is that even as he started to lose sight due to cataracts, an opacity of the eye's lens that develops with age, his mental vision never wavered. He went nearly blind yet wearing glasses with various tints, continued to paint his vision of fleeting effects of light and atmosphere. As Dr. Howard Markel asserts in his profile of Monet for PBS Hour, "To those of us who have so-called perfect sight, or perhaps are a bit myopic, the water lilies are still masterpieces of vision, no matter what eye condition Monet suffered."

Visual and color disturbances resulted in different versions of Monet's vision that endures. In this book, you are privy to my own vision that I hope endures, too!

I learned the power of sight while working at Johnson & Johnson Vision (formerly Vistakon and Vision Care) for fifteen years. We may take them for granted, but our eyes capture light from the world around us and send visual information to our brains. Vision is the most used sense of all. Eyes can represent a gateway into the soul, intelligence, light, vigilance, moral conscience, and truth. Looking someone in the eye may be interpreted as a gesture of honesty.

Eyes can see hundreds of colors in varying shades full of potential and possibilities. Long ago, I started to think of my journey with this view. Open and advocating for all the colors of humans, supporting their potential and possibilities so we could all elevate. Helping brands create experiences through their products and services that make others feel connected and uplifted. I maintained this lens over the course of corporate landscapes that each position brought.

Senses and emotions are strongly interrelated with experiences. The most prolific experiences are authentic, remain in the memory and change human notions by provoking emotions and feelings and allowing people to participate and be involved.

The adage around love and dating is that "men are visual creatures", which does not track with the fact that women drive 70-80% of all consumer purchasing decisions. We're all visual creatures in the Experience Era. The visual, what we see, is the cue for what is real in front of us.

As I was entering my final years in corporate America, I had a powerful vision. It was no longer a point of view or designer frame with accents. As bright as a burst of crimson, I saw myself helping others become more visible and elevating them to their highest potential. Over my career, I had seen what it was like to provide minorities with a seat at the table so they could be seen on equal footing with their white counterparts and win contracts based on their capabilities and potential. I had watched these individuals and their companies compete and excel over others with more resources when given the proper guidance and support. And I had seen the exponential effect these entities would have on their families, companies, and communities based on jobs their efforts created, the increased education their families were provided, and the improvement in their livelihoods. It became clear that I was going to define something that would allow me to pass on the many gifts of insight and support I had received over the years and do so in a fashion that would have a ripple effect on those around me.

The spirit of that vision reverberated within me for the next decade. Upon retirement, I launched my brand, SEE Company—blending my love for retail, my passion for diversity and inclusion, and my desire to create a sustainable company that gives back more than it takes. A brand that will See Everyone Elevate™, championing causes while making beautiful products for consumers.

But you see, looking the part is not enough (even though I do love clothes). In believing it, we're almost there. Therefore, SEE Company is governed by the following values, which are fundamental to *See and Believe*:

Be your best self.

Enrich well-being.

Live your purpose.

Inspire and innovate.

Elevate through challenges.

Value everyone.

Everyone gives and grows.

If we always go further to elevate, the collective story will be something, a dazzling spectacle, our eyes have never seen before. Reflections in and of themselves hold valuable stories and lessons. I'll go first and tell you mine.

It is my greatest desire for *See and Believe* to be your lifetime companion for an elevated perspective on life and business. Let's help each other see more. A world transformed by so much color and light may be only one vision away.

—*Bev Jennings*

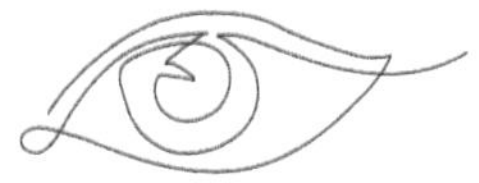

Chapter 1

Inspirational First Sights

"It's not what you look at that matters, it's what you see."

—HENRY DAVID THOREAU,
NATURALIST AND ESSAYIST

GROWING UP IN the country helps you develop a life-long appreciation of the land, animals, fresh vegetables, and how to be resourceful. There were many adventures in the fields, forests, and creeks. As far as the eye could see, people were picking peas and cotton. I also remember my mother saying, "It's not where you come from. It's where you want to go." I would never forget those words through ages and seasons. Rural life showed me that we didn't have much in material abundance, but we had so much—love, attention, safety, enrichment, confidence, family role models for business and entrepreneurship, and I dare say, hard labor skills when necessary.

In my family, I was one of four children. I had two older brothers and one older sister. We grew up in Greenwood, Florida, an hour from Tallahassee, which is farmland. My parents worked at Florida State Hospital. My mom was a nurse's aide. My dad was a barber. They were also small business owners in their trade with a country store and a nightclub (or "juke joint"), and farmers. We were into sustainability—supporting ecological, human, and economic health and vitality—long before they called it "sustainability".

My mom and dad were a great team. This doesn't mean they stayed together forever. They divorced when I was twelve. But I learned the concept of teamwork first from them. My dad would make us all breakfast because my mom was already hard at work. Then she always directed dinner while he was at work. When it came to us kids, they were united and aligned. You couldn't play the game of one parent against the other! My grandmother, as middle manager, came in every day behind them and cleaned up our mess. And she was paid. My grandfather was very creative in his businesses. He owned over 200 acres of land. He even donated the land the Greenwood Chapel Church was built on. That church is still on the land. He did endure health issues and lived on our property in a little room in between the barber shop and store. He had both of his legs amputated due to diabetes, but he kept demonstrating his many abilities even as his health declined. With his bubbly personality, he added humor and a different point of view to the team.

I loved wearing my sister's clothes. I was honored. In contrast, my brother refused to wear our older brother's clothes. I couldn't understand that. It made me happy to wear hand-me-downs! If these clothes were fashionable for Debra, she set the example for me. I could demonstrate individuality while adorning myself with something she originally chose to show her beauty, contours and personality.

I attended an all-Black school until the eighth grade, then a larger, integrated one throughout high school. Early on, business was at the heart of all this education in tandem with understanding how diverse people functioned together. Funny, the term, *diversity*, was never spoken in those times, but I was well-aware of its power. I no longer wanted to be in an all-Black school or all-white one for that matter. I loved the variety of perspectives and appearances of my assorted friends and teachers.

People used to look up to our family like we were well-to-do. We were not. I don't know how my parents got it right, but they were fantastic role models. As if she replicated herself to function past the twenty-four clock, my mother was present for every school event, every picnic without ever dropping the ball in her variety of jobs. She was insistent on higher education. The words, "You will go to college", were said often. They couldn't afford to send us, but we were expected to attend and do well somehow, and I didn't disappoint. I went to University of West Florida for my undergrad, Chipola College in Marianna, and later completed my MBA at University of Dallas.

When I think of what's gotten me where I am today, it's a composite of all those experiences of what I witnessed as a child and through today, my vision of seeing everyone elevate. My parents were minority business owners with immense work ethic between them. They didn't just maintain one job. The four of us kids were certainly another job. Our aspirations were front and center, not our color, but that doesn't mean that race did not inform some of my experiences.

Seeing Culture, Not Color

Living in light skin is a conversation starter. When we were traveling together recently, I discussed this topic with my brother. Corporate America could see my skin as "black", but we were talking to my cousin, and she made the comment about our light skin, thinking in the lived experience of tones. Our brother and sister who passed away were darker. We read about light-skinned Blacks being treated differently both inside and outside the culture. I asked if he felt a difference. He did. I did, too. We were teased as children but didn't think much about it until this spirited road trip all these years later.

I can remember a bus driver taking us to public school, and I was probably three shades lighter than I am. I'm always bubbly and friendly. I said, "Good morning," and he would reply, "Good morning, Red!"

I never took that negatively even as the laughter on the bus got louder. It never bothered me. The tone didn't hold me back or push me forward. There is such a thin layer that is your skin, and we're all the same underneath it. It's so thin you wonder how it can determine so much. It's unbelievable how that can have such an impact. Call it me being naïve or not making the body's external surface, an organ we all have, more than that (which is a lot), but I have always looked beyond skin.

Every time a Black or white person says, "I don't see color," they are criticized with skepticism, like, "*Of course, you do!*" Well, the reality is, can you see more than color? See beyond skin. Have a desire to get to know someone based on their culture. How did you grow up? Where did you come from? If you peel back the onion, those experiences shape our lives forever. That's what you want to know. Every person is a sum of many experiences, which are embedded in culture and make it cumulative, always progressing.

How do I describe myself? I always start by saying, "I am a woman." Then I'm an African American woman and I am mixed heritage. I am a woman of faith. The reality is when it comes to culture, it's such an evolution. Over time, culture happens to you, but you don't know it happens to you until you get an opportunity to reflect. It's experiences first and foremost. There is family and education. You can't see culture. You see color, and people tend to go after what they can see. There's nothing wrong with that, but if we could see in a way that we want to see everyone elevate, and have a perspective of elevation vs. difference, honor the differences because none of us are the same anyway until you peel back that skin layer. This could make a world of difference as to who we are and how we are.

Culture does matter. In Greenwood, Florida, a rural area, the culture is that people just drop by to visit. All of a sudden, a car pulls up in your yard. They get out, ring the doorbell or knock, and they expect you to let them in for coffee, cookies and chat or wine time. This is something I miss in the land of security officers and gates. Very different worlds—and I embrace them all.

The common thread that runs through all of us is relationships. Relationships matter in this life regardless of geography, skin tones, jobs you're in or not, country clubs you belong to or not. All of us will reach that point in our lives, the last few minutes, and all those things will not matter. Relationships are why we are here. If we are here doing the highest good for the time we are granted and what we do with that time, it comes down to how we operate within those relationships. Are we helping each other? Are we making a difference?

I did an internship for a savings and loan company. This provided early insights about managing finances. My first fulltime job was as management trainee for JC Penney Co. in Pensacola. That was my first job after I graduated from college at the age of twenty, early for a lot but I was eager to work! I went to college through the summers. At JCP, I was the only African American woman in management and rather young starting out, but I had a very supportive boss. Then I got married (another chapter and another lens from which to see life!) and moved to help start up a store in New Bern, North Carolina, which is known for its historic homes and grand gardens. I started as a trainee, then became a buyer. I've always been in management and surrounded by solid role models mainly consisting of white men. After all, they were the bodies and brains in the actual roles. I possessed a great comfort level in supervising white men because that's how I started. I literally didn't know any other way to be.

When I first started with Johnson & Johnson, having relocated from Fort Worth, Texas, I rented a car and stopped at a gas station. I knew I was back in the South. When we grew up, we had white neighbors who were considered extended family. On this morning, there was no feeling of family. I was pumping gas and I heard one guy utter the word, "nigger". His eyes had laser-beamed on skin color, unearthing hateful teachings that caused empty hate to spew from his mouth. It didn't mean anything to me but a display of ignorance, a face that wasn't welcoming me to my lovely home state of Florida.

Later, in my first role as warehouse supervisor at Johnson & Johnson Vision Care, one of my guys,

Mark, entered my office. A hard worker with a gentle soul, his red face twisted in a wave of pain. I thought he had been injured or something had happened in his family. I showed concern and inquired, "What's wrong, Mark?"

His lips quivered and he said, "They called me a nigger lover and accused me of sucking up to you."

I chuckled and said, "Really? Where's the nigger?"

Mark went from crying to laughing. He thought I would be upset because I was their supervisor. I never had another overt experience like that. Word spread that I was fair. I never chased down the mouth that spewed this hateful word. My intention was to make Mark feel more comfortable. He really wanted to defend me, but I also knew that he spent a lot of time with his peer group and my reaction would dictate the days and weeks ahead for him. As Mark's manager, I had to do the highest good for him. Doing the highest good is a value that would set the pace and trajectory of every day of my life and allow me to see and believe breathtaking acts of humankind, leadership, and brand elevation.

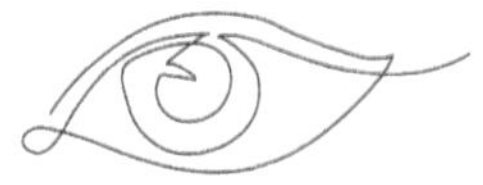

Chapter 2

Choose Your Lens

"When fear rushed in, I learned how to hear my heart racing but refused to allow my feelings to sway me. That resilience came from my family. It flowed through our bloodline."

—Coretta Scott King,
AUTHOR AND CIVIL RIGHTS LEADER

MY MOTHER WAS ninety when she died of dementia. When we discovered that she was suffering from this debilitating disease, it was clear she had been hiding it. My brother called me to share that she had gotten lost after driving on the wrong side of the road. Praise God she did not have an accident before a police officer escorted her to the station. Dementia slowly ate away at her life for ten years. We all took good care of her, which extended her life. I feel fortunate that she knew who I was, her doting daughter, for most of that time.

Having been a nurse's aide for many years, she followed some of the protocol she used to take care of others to help take care of herself even as she was deteriorating.

Perhaps also wanting to spare us any "trouble", as he would deem our fuss over him, my dad kept his failing health private and died of liver cancer at the age of sixty-seven. The wisdom from my parents seeps into many of my decisions and acts. With their lives so varied, they demonstrated that wisdom comes in countless forms as long as our minds are open to it.

In his book, *Simple Truths*, Kent Nerburn writes, "There are many ways to seek wisdom. There is travel, there are masters, there is service. There is staring into the eyes of children and elders and lovers and strangers. There is sitting silently in one spot and there is being swept along in life's turbulent current. Life itself will grant you wisdom in ways you may neither understand nor choose. It is up to you to be open to all these sources of wisdom and to embrace them with your whole heart."

With this writing, Kent Nerburn will know that I've sought a great deal of wisdom from him in the pages of his books! In fact, we share a few values. He states, "My work has been a constant search, from various perspectives, for an authentic American spirituality, integrating our western Judeo-Christian tradition with the other traditions of the world, and especially the indigenous spirituality of the people who first inhabited this continent. Someone once called me a 'guerilla theologian', and I think that is fairly accurate. I am deeply concerned with the human condition and our responsibility to the earth, the people on it, and the generations to come. I believe that we are, at heart, spiritual beings seeking spiritual meaning, and I try to honor this search in my work and my daily life. If there is a quote I live by, it is the entreaty of the Lakota Chief, Sitting Bull, who said to the U.S. government that was trying to eradicate his people, 'Come, let us put our minds together to see what kind of life we can create for our children.'"

This quote is a study on filling your bucket from the well of fresh wisdom life grants us.

Elevate Through Challenges to Be Your Best Self

Okay, founders, leaders, and everyday extraordinary individuals, let's say you see the well of wisdom shimmering before you, but you're not sure if you can learn and grow from it. You're in pain, at a crossroads and indecisive, or just lost a loved one. Challenges help define us through our next thoughts and actions. Your mind will either lead you to that well for wisdom that will elevate you or close the door to learning and elevation.

Dr. Carol Dweck coined the terms, *fixed mindset,* and *growth mindset,* to describe the underlying beliefs people have about learning and intelligence. Dweck found in her research that one of the most basic beliefs we carry about ourselves has to do with how we view and inhabit what we consider to be personality. A "fixed mindset" assumes that character, intelligence, and creative ability are static attributes which we can't change in any meaningful way, and success is the affirmation of that inherent intelligence, an assessment of how those attributes are the benchmark for an equally fixed standard; striving for success and avoiding failure at all costs become a way of maintaining the sense of being smart or skilled.

A "growth mindset", in contrast, thrives on challenge and sees failure not as evidence of unintelligence but as a heartening springboard for growth and for maximizing our existing abilities. Out of these two mindsets, which we manifest from a very early age, springs a great deal of our behavior, our relationship with success and failure in both professional and personal contexts, and ultimately, our capacity for happiness. Dweck found that at the heart of what makes growth mindset a winning proposition is that it creates a passion for learning rather than a hunger for approval. Adopting this mindset will not only decrease your worries of being discouraged by failure, but Dweck's research tells us you are unlikely to see yourself as failing in hard situations; you will see yourself as learning. Human qualities such as creativity and intelligence, and even love and connection, can be cultivated through effort and intentional practice.

Being in pursuit of a growth mindset will help you strengthen courage because it *rewards* individuals for what they don't know. The words, "I don't know", turns a lack of knowledge into an opportunity for improvement that will be cumulative toward best self. At present, you lack the knowledge or skills but you're willing to work to acquire them.

My dear friend and a spiritual coach Patricia Hill, who was with me through my brand journey, has shared that we have wakeup calls along the way that help us understand cycles and patterns. She designed a program taking people through their story and helping them identify and learn from. These imprints from childhood experience, beliefs that loved ones handed down, which we internalized but didn't consciously choose, are detailed in the storyline. If we have a growth mindset and consider the storyline, we can reach for highest self and feel what our highest self wants so that we don't repeat patterns.

Being our best self truly requires us to know where we come from and own our story. Owning it doesn't require sharing it like I am for the world to see and believe, but it means having awareness of all the parts and inner workings. Family is a substantial ingredient in the smorgasbord of SELF.

My cousin, Doris, offers a window, an example of how family shaped the story of Beverly Jennings and carved out imprints, as Patricia Hill shares how to understand, learn from and elevate. With Doris's "Light Lessons" and the others to come, I leave the integrity of their words without drastically chopping and shaping, which would put my lens on their gracious stories and tips for elevating.

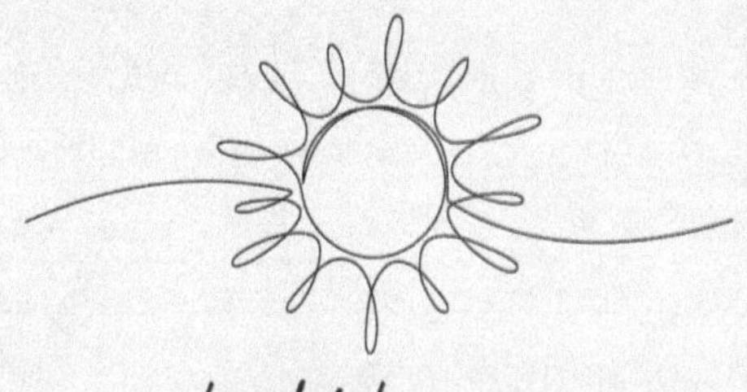

Doris Dickens On Elevating Ancestral Wisdom

Staircases are inundated with individuals trying to reach the ceiling by any means possible, but few make it. For some like Bev, it's almost impossible. In fact, I think Bev was able reach the ceiling and consequently, is a great leader because she is naturally ambitious, courageous, and disciplined with an unwavering faith in God; because she has the vision, foresight and more importantly, the fortitude to keep climbing in spite of any obstacles, adversity or naysayers; and because she inherited a unique business sense from her father and grandfather who were courageous, creative and unwavering in the plight to build and sustain successful businesses.

Lastly, and more importantly, I believe Bev was able to reach the ceiling at J&J and become a great leader because she excelled from one level to the next while remaining humbled and ambitious. She had the foresight to seek out mentor(s) and to continue to sharpen her perspectives, knowledge, and skills by engaging in continuous education and/ or lifelong learning both mentally and spiritually. Every time I spoke to her, she was reading a book, or participating in a leadership seminar, workshop or spiritual retreat.

Napoleon Hill said, "If you can conceive it and believe it, you can achieve it." To see and believe is to be able to not only envision it but be able to anticipate the hurdles and obstacles you will face and still have a belief so strong that it can overcome any perceived obstacles and adversity.

Just do it! But you also don't get to be there unless you possess integrity, discipline, self-actualization and the courage to make it.

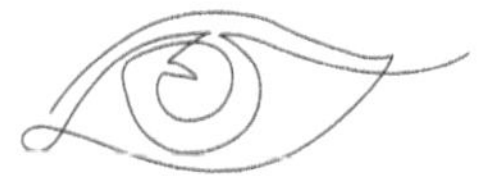

Chapter 3

Seeing Me Elevate

"Doing is a quantum leap from imagining."

—Barbara Sher,
self-improvement coach

IN THE GOODS and services universe of Johnson & Johnson, there were thousands of brands. One uniform thing that resonated with all of us, however, was our credo, values that guide 130,000 employees. A former J&J CEO said: "The credo is the heart of Johnson & Johnson, and you can't live without a heart." It zeroed in on the importance of values and stating your values.

Johnson & Johnson's credo guided me for thirty-two years. My last position was as head of supplier diversity, allowing me to work across 250 operating companies around the globe. Prior to this, I was VP for Consumer Group and process excellence working with the companies' CEO. I certified master black belts on process

23

improvement in the consumer business—for example, Neutrogena and Baby Products. What amazing experiences I had. I had an opportunity to work on the largest acquisition, Pfizer Consumer Healthcare, and lead integration for it in North America.

It wasn't a perfect journey, but it was the robust and positive direction toward seeing and believing the brand that is my reality and passion today. As head of global supplier diversity and inclusion, I worked with thousands of business owners, those underrepresented in corporate America, and it allowed me to inform their business.

As consumers, we buy products that complement and enhance our quality of life, but we may not think about the suppliers toiling over each part and ingredient to make them whole. It's more fascinating and wisdom-rich than you can imagine! At least from my position. For instance, there are differences in capabilities for suppliers in how they can support a giant corporation. What suppliers may not understand is that it's never one person making decisions. It's a team.

There were times I questioned why one supplier would get the business over another. My role was one of influence. We built in the inclusion of diverse suppliers so they could get an RFP (request for proposal) or RFI (request for information). We tried to include at least one, if not more. Now they could bid and at least compete for business at that point.

We wrote in guidelines. We got creative in some of the bigger ones partnering with minority-owned businesses. We never acquiesced on our standards. All suppliers were held to the same standards. I couldn't tell you it was always fair because relationships, history, pricing, cost, quality and service considerations factored into the equation.

I coached them, but I couldn't give any competitive advantage. Without treating a larger one unfairly, I gave guidance. There were times they complained. If I thought the complaint was legitimate, I addressed it with the category leader, chief procurement officer, their team of VPs. I never turned my back on a complaint. I always addressed it. The goal was to follow the credo and live with those values.

Navigating these partnerships was tough and eye-opening across the categories of spend. We had over thirty categories and within those, we could have as many as twenty subcategories. I needed to be able to field questions, sit toe to toe with the category leaders, understand their part of the business and straddle between the leaders and the business owners who owned the budget. Being able to influence the business across 250 operating companies with differing levels of business maturity and not everyone had a strong company. Imagine the breadth of that—understanding what's going on in the business while selling brands and adding new brands. It was massive. No one could fake the brainpower required. You had to get in there, immerse and understand what the business was going through and leadership accountabilities. I worked on the consumer side too, managing relationships with Walmart, CVS and others and their supplier programs, making sure we were helping them meet their second-tier goals. I spent a lot of time on the hospital side visiting with our salespeople fostering those relationships with the largest hospitals, GPOs (group purchasing organizations), as well as the other side of the business. You had to also be able to work internally and externally, uplifting the reputation of Johnson & Johnson in the marketplace, with the patients, customers and consumers. It was being authentic and true to all of that, being able to move in the different circles with different people and update the executives at the top on our "healthy futures" goals worldwide we committed to. The aspect that was most important was the relationships.

I have long been an advocate of diversity and inclusion but back in the mid 1990s internally, we called it *affirmative action*. I remember being honored for this by the J&J CEO at the corporate headquarters, along with four others in the corporation. My proud (and well-dressed!) mom was my guest. The memory of that evening has always stayed with me. I thought how special to be honored for leading by example for what was a part of me—respect for all people—in front of the person who first showed me this. Receiving that award, I saw and felt what it meant to include and recognize women, people of color, people with disabilities, and individuals of the LGBT community in every phase of the business—so much so that I embraced this approach in every executive leadership position I held for the next thirty years of my professional career.

Believing in Advocacy

Later, I started the Women's Leadership Initiative at J&J Vision. We had employee resource groups (ERG), showing we were somewhat ahead of the curve, but I wanted the adoption rate to be better so people felt that equity and belonging. That they could be who they are. I wanted that for everybody. That is why when you have strong core beliefs, when things are falling around you, you can stand on that. When you can stand on that, you have hope. Hope brings courage. You can see that future ahead. If you feel your contribution is making a difference and you belong, you stay.

The women's group for Johnson & Johnson Vision Care was the first time I went all in. I wanted to see more movement. We held our first event seven years later, and two of the executive committee members came to show their support. It was a big deal to bring in Gail Blanke, president and CEO of Lifedesigns, a company whose mission is to empower women worldwide, to keynote. Once you've taken a stand, your brand changes. I was personally and professionally shifting with this advocacy add-on, you could say, then in the role in consumer companies working across sixty companies with their boards. Busy time!

I was at J&J Vision for fifteen years. Then when I moved to Consumer Group, I co-led the African American ERG. I've been advocating for employees while working with executives to really pave the way for fairness to make sure women and Blacks were represented and advancing. I and other ERG leaders worked with the chief diversity office to elevate programs and open eyes now that mine were more open.

I co-led the African American ERG for ten years. When I tell people I worked eighty-hour weeks, they don't believe me. There were times when it was a show to get attention and engagement. Are we making a difference though? Doing the highest good? There were so many times I felt like others weren't listening. We needed a healthy balance too though, elevating all groups and not just one. Disappointment never caused me to be less committed or give up.

One boss actually told me, "You need to lighten up on your African American employee resource group efforts because it can affect your career." He was concerned because he saw something from another level that I couldn't. I could tell he was uncomfortable mentioning it. I believed in what I was doing, and I stood on my own personal values fused with the credo values. Later, it paid off.

When I began, my group had ranked at the bottom

within J&J when it came to supplier diversity. I galvanized my team around sourcing and developing companies that were representative of the diversity and inclusion principles the companies wanted to exemplify. During that period, the group went from last place to first place in supplier diversity. This focus and dedication helped J&J become the first health care company to join the Billion Dollar Roundtable, a member corporation group that spends more than a billion dollars annually with certified veteran, LGBT, disabled, women, and minority businesses. In doing so, it helped generate over $1.7 billion annually in spend with diverse suppliers, experience 70% growth, and $3 billion annually in spend with small businesses under my leadership.

How was all this possible?

From 1988 to 2019, you have thirty years of ebbs and flows of progress for women and minorities. When half of your employees are outside the US who don't understand this need, it's slow moving. Then we had a lot of employees relocating to the US, and with that migration, brought more comprehension and progress. Minds opened with the assortment of talent informed by different cultures.

In that colorful season, I developed a louder voice. I rode on the corporate jet. I traveled with the executive committee. The CFO said to me, "Bev, you moved the consumer group from last place to first place in process excellence. I commend you for your leadership."

With performance reviews, there were times I was

disappointed, and others tried to shade my narrative. Some people who didn't know me thought I was advocating for others to advance myself. That was never the case. Someone must have the courage to step out and speak up even if you're putting your own career at risk.

I'm grateful for my J&J experience because I know I wouldn't have the fortitude and dedication to go on with my life's work had it not been for the lives that touched me and that I touched during my career at J & J. It really left a mark that will be with me until I leave this earth. How many people can see the impact that a corporation has had on them?

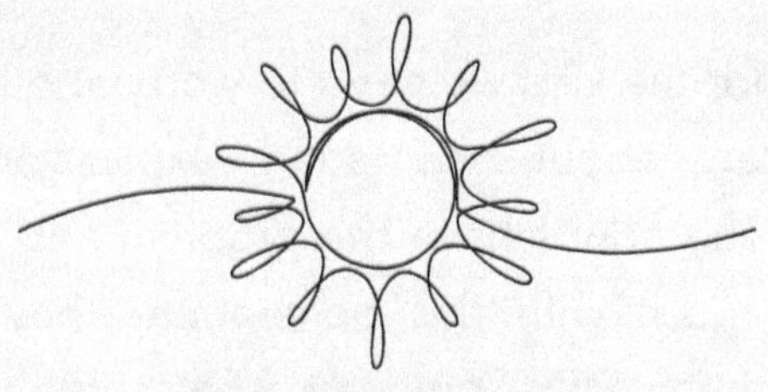

Light Lessons

Necole Neal On Elevating Trust

I was right out of college when I met Beverly. I went in for an interview and we clicked. There was something about us together that has always clicked no matter what business venture we're into. I was young, twenty-four years old when I walked into the room. She walked in as a force, a velvet hammer.

She could tell me we're starting another brand, and I say, "Let's go!" That level of mutual trust has made my role all-inclusive. We protect the brand and take pride in our work that is grounded in the values of diversity and inclusion for everyone.

We all have to figure out how we express our feelings about diversity and inclusion. Some of us are quieter in how we support it. Wearing clothes by a brand that stands for this rather than wearing big words on your chest is a big deal. The whole atmosphere of intolerance is disheartening. I have kids in high school and college whose tolerance and acceptance of everyone exactly where they are is amazing. It's world changing.

It's not the kids we need to worry about. They don't care about orientation, expression, pronouns. The adults have the problem and they're out of touch with this generation—they're not seeing them. SEE Company represents this generation. We brainstorm for so long and it doesn't have to be one race. It's everyone. It's simple. Why overcomplicate it? Sometimes they can't vocalize it for whatever reason, but at least they can wear it. They may be the only ones that know it, but they are expressing it through these beautiful clothes.

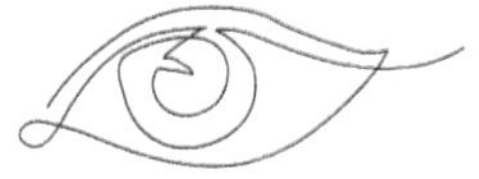

Chapter 4

Branding Is Believing

"Everyone has a purpose in life and a unique talent to give to others. And when we blend this unique talent with service to others, we experience the ecstasy and exultation of own spirit, which is the ultimate goal of all goals."

—KALLAM ANJI REDDY,
ENTREPRENEUR

IN 2006, I attended Life Mastery by Tony Robbins, in the Fiji Islands. In this Namale paradise before even forming a thought, let alone an intentionally transformative one, the dreamy blue sea and white sand beaches are a role model for mastery! That was such a pivotal period for me taking the time out of an eighty-hour workweek to cleanse, refresh and replenish all of me. I really challenged myself about my life purpose. Am I leaning into this when I'm making a decision? Does it align with my life's purpose?

Thereafter, I embarked on obtaining a certification in master business coaching with Fowler School of Business. I wanted to enable myself to be a better coach. There were many useful takeaways that I still use today in my services business. The best gem of all is that I paired with another participant who interviewed me and wrote my story in 2015. In that story, I talked about what would become SEE Company, as well as building a beach home. The power of story. It was already truth before the full manifestation. It was also a story of knowing your worth and asking for it, which reminds me of the first example of this that defined me.

While working for a Sara Lee company, I was having a conversation with my office mate (white female) who had less responsibility and experience than I did. She told me what her salary was, and I could not believe the difference—she was making thousands of dollars more. My first instinct was to go straight to HR. However, I did not because we were not supposed to share personal information, and I did not want to get her in trouble. Perhaps I was already doing the highest good.

One evening of many, I was working late, and our president dropped by my office. He asked how things were going. I decided it was my moment to convey my situation in a respectful and authentic way. I knew my worth, and I knew that I deserved equal pay. It was my responsibility to ask for it. I never brought race into the conversation (although unconscious/conscious bias may have been a factor); only equity for the role and contributions made. He resolved the inequity. He showed integrity, which was instrumental to this story.

I'm a person of high integrity. I have a mantra in my life that guides me. I challenged myself when making major decisions to live my life purpose. I shared it with my grand retirement party at J&J. I had it printed on sustainable coasters made of wood. During my farewell speech, I talked about the highest intention and purpose in my life: *Give love, enjoy life, do the highest good.* Etched on the back, "Bev Jennings 2019, Johnson & Johnson". It's become an artifact. People I connect to still have this as guidance for themselves.

At the retirement party, which took place at their colossal museum, half of the executive committee attended. One of the monumental moments was when one of the executive committee members said, "We know you wanted us to go faster and how difficult it was for you to advance diversity and inclusion. We weren't there yet, but you made a significant difference. You see where we are today." Those words fed all my senses and capped my thirty years of fighting for equity within the corporate landscape.

Retirement was bittersweet. I had many emotions running through me. I was reminded of Helen Keller's words, "Keep your face to the sunshine and you cannot see the shadow." Time to look forward. Time to see bright possibilities and be overtaken by them and not succumb to fear and negativity.

Talk about an icon that defied the odds. Helen Keller was afflicted at the age of nineteen months with an illness (possibly scarlet fever) that left her blind and deaf. She was examined by Alexander Graham Bell at the age of six. As a result, he sent to her a twenty-year-old teacher, Anne Sullivan (Macy) from the Perkins Institution for the Blind in Boston, which Bell's son-in-law directed. Sullivan, a remarkable teacher, remained with Keller from March 1887 until her own death in October 1936. Within months, Keller had learned to feel objects and associate them with words spelled out by finger signals on her palm, to read sentences by feeling raised words on cardboard, and to make her own sentences by arranging words in a frame. During 1888–90 she spent winters at the Perkins Institution learning Braille. Then she began a slow process of learning to speak under Sarah Fuller of the Horace Mann School for the Deaf, also in Boston. She also learned to lip-read by placing her fingers on the lips and throat of the speaker while the words were simultaneously spelled out for her.

After learning about such a life, how could we not see and believe our own wonderous potential?

It reminds me of when my niece, Desiree, was pregnant with her first child and she and her husband visited me in New Jersey while they were in the process of relocating to New York. They were still deciding on what to name their daughter. The couple asked me to tell them about my father, their grandfather, and his siblings. I happily shared but I inadvertently omitted my Aunt Lula. Then I remembered. I boasted that she was beautifully disabled and resilient. She was blind. They both exclaimed, "Oh my goodness. We will name her Lula!" Lula will be thirteen years old this year, and both she and her younger sister, Brisana, are beautiful, strong, and resilient.

Live Your Purpose

On my retirement anniversary, I had a palm tree planted outside my new office (my home office). The tree symbolizes new beginnings.

That tree sparked me to visualize. Visualization is a key factor in manifesting change by enabling us to craft a clear mental image of our goals. Vividly imagining our desired outcome lays the groundwork for its realization, aligning our thoughts and actions toward that goal. This process taps into our subconscious, fostering purpose, motivation, and determination to turn that mental image into reality.

Tree planted and vision starting to form, I was onto fulfilling purpose without the walls and resources of a multinational corporation!

Richard J. Leider is the founder of Inventure—The Purpose Company, whose mission is to help people unlock the power of purpose. Widely viewed as a pioneer of the global purpose movement, Leider has written or cowritten eleven books, including three bestsellers, which have sold over one million copies. His latest, *Who Do You Want to Be*

When You Grow Old?: The Path of Purposeful Aging, speaks to the moment, the big transition I was in. He writes, "Grow old on purpose. Navigate a purposeful path from adulthood to elderhood with choice, curiosity, and courage. Everyone is getting old; not everyone is growing old. But the path of purposeful aging is accessible to all—and it's fundamental to health, happiness, and longevity."

Knowing the power purpose held, I had to uphold the belief in mine that started in my professional framework. I had total freedom. Delicious, dangerous freedom. Decisions and missteps were all mine for a change.

The psychology of belief is a powerful tool that has a significant impact on motivation. When you believe in yourself and your ability to achieve your goals, you are more likely to take action and overcome obstacles along the way. Your belief in your own potential and the belief that your goals are attainable can fuel your motivation to work hard and persevere. Without belief, motivation can wane, and it becomes easy to give up on your goals. However, when you have a strong belief in yourself and your abilities, you are more likely to stay committed and dedicated to achieving your goals, even when faced with challenges.

A Brand-New Brand World

Brands were not immersive experiences when I walked through the doors of my first retail job. It was product speak, not brand as an emotional concept rooted in human perception, emotion, attitudes, and beliefs. With purpose, I had to reflect now that I had the time and get clear on my understanding of a brand and how successful mine could be in this brand-new brand world!

The truth is, successful brands are no longer marketing at a consumer, they are building a relationship with an audience. Consumers, and particularly from the "Gens" after Gen X, expect more from corporations and companies. Brands must stimulate them, foster collaborative partnerships in their life endeavors, be good stewards of diversity, equity, inclusion, and justice, and personalize the experience of making a brand stick in minds, yes, but ultimately, hearts. Brand immersion. Are they speaking to the needs, desires, and causes at point of purchase? If so, attraction leads to attachment in the new cycle of *immersive experience*.

I now understood brand to be about desire, drama, and dollar signs.

Emotion is a four-part process consisting of physiological arousal, cognitive interpretation, subjective feelings, and behavioral expression. We also possess logic and practical wisdom, of course, driving what we say and how we behave, but emotion engages us in an experience and relationship. If, as psychologists and neuroscientists say, "we are all here for love and belonging", how we connect is core to our lived experience and where our money goes. Brands that stand the test of time stand for more than their price tag. I think about how even with pharmaceutical products, medical devices, consumer products, professional endorsement used to matter. Now, celebrity endorsements and social media greatly influence consumer purchasing decisions. Both serve to implant a desire that even starts to feel like a need or must-have. Anyone can make a video, but does it have imagination?

Brand expert and "idea whisperer" Mitch Markson wrote and drew and photographed the book, *The Imagination Playbook*, a guide to help you be more imaginative, playful, and purposeful with your brand, whether that brand is you, your product/service, your organization, or an identifying issue you are passionate about. Inside, you learn how to feel more comfortable with the designations of Imagination and Creativity and find and flex your imagination and creativity muscles with "playtime" activities, imagination-stirring tools, not rules, a personal branding guide, and a social issue-to-brand primer with plenty of examples. To trigger your ideas, he recommends listing five to ten things that stimulate your imagination, such as dreams and nightmares, graffiti or street art, movies, and five to ten idealists who inspire you, such as inventive writer and filmmaker, Guillermo Del Toro. Who inspires you?

Having conceived and designed so many brands, Mitch wrote this book as a gift proselytizing the power of a major asset we all start to develop before the age of two! Albert Einstein said, "Logic will get you from A to B. Imagination will take you everywhere."

When you think about your brand, don't forget to imagine. Start with something familiar: color. A compact jewel of a book called *Color, Form, and Magic* breaks down the symbolism, meanings, historical references, and feelings that colors evoke. If you want your brand to convey intensity and strength, for example, red may be a natural choice. "It can increase your respiration just by looking at it!" That *is* intense. The book goes on to list key words (two words that are integral to branding in this always-online world), such as action, motivation, danger, lust, and fire. Now, envision red. What do you see? Does it color in your brand?

All these components are extensive, and they're meant to be exhaustive for a brand to sustain and elevate.

Conceiving SEE Company

When I thought of my company name almost a decade ago, I couldn't act on it, but I kept it on my vision board. See: See Entrepreneurs Elevate.

I hired an outstanding designer and brand guru to help me clarify. It was the hardest work I've ever done. Yes, that's right. While homing in on capabilities and making a marketing video, I struggled. I was surprised I struggled.

I pushed through my fears during the video shoot for my website. It was at the height of the pandemic and the makeup artist and videographer were the first persons outside of family I had allowed into my home during the pandemic. I was full of anxiety but knew that to SEE it, I had to step into it!

In leaving this corporate world and becoming an entrepreneur, you're changing your identity, and you don't even realize it because you're so caught up in who you've been and you're operating within a familiar ecosystem. Then when you start a brand, you're kind of lost but you soon wake up like, *wait, I've got this!* After all, in my career, I had some step-up "startups" where I was the leader, ranging from a 1979 JC Penney new store, distribution for the global launch of Acuvue, a manufacturing line, and the gargantuan J&J Consumer Pfizer Consumer Healthcare Acquisition Integration. As I reflect, these startups enabled me with experience, confidence, and courage to take on the next one— my own.

It comes down to the decision to start. A decision is powerful and exhilarating. The universe rides with you when you're intentional. That pull of energy is a force. You don't have all the answers, but you're moving. Movement is palpable. Best laid plans may not work out, but you must be willing to adapt and adopt. Make the moves when you need to make the moves. It's all about making decisions, moving forward. The road isn't always clear. If you really want to see everyone elevate, it takes the courage to keep moving.

Making a brand takes years. It's all about what you believe. Take those values and let it be a compass for your business and your life. When you have clarity around your North Star, you can challenge yourself without flailing or taking a detour. You can accentuate, but the core remains the same. It's like decorating a Christmas tree.

In my brand work, it was time to pull out the colorful lights. It dawned on me that if entrepreneurs aren't elevating their people, what good is it? Then I changed it to SEE Company: See Everyone Elevate™. It walked the talk of inclusivity. I wanted to make sure that came through loud and clear. There is power in a name, but when a name has a special meaning, it gives it energy it wouldn't otherwise have.

I must confess, and thanks to David Ogunrinde, for stellar inquiry on the brand's identity, there is also an inspirational person embedded in SEE Company. (I hope she will be flattered to know!)

David asked during one of our long brainstorming sessions in a conference room, "If SEE were a person, who would SEE be?"

After a long pause, I said, "I have to think about that."

We were trying to narrow down the brand attributes. I sounded off, "Gayle King!" Necole gasped and asked why. That was 2019. I had just retired. The story goes, a couple of years prior, I was at the Kentucky Derby in the mansion, and Gayle and I were both guests of host Rohena Miller. My contact lens got stuck in my eye and I was in the ladies' room, where there were makeup artists and other celebs. Gayle rushed over to me and insisted that she try to get it out. "When Oprah got her contact lens stuck in her eye, I could help…" and right then, the optometrist came in wide-eyed.

I heard Gayle King speak a couple of times. I respect her. Can you imagine your best friend being Oprah? The person who always draws attention. I love her vibrant colors that she's not afraid to know. She has inspired the SEE brand. Gayle tried to help me see that day!

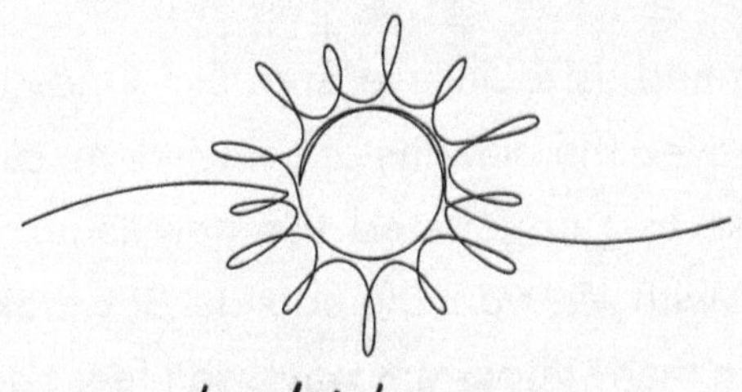

Light Lessons

David Ogunrinde On Elevating Identity

You know that rare feeling, when someone shows up to hold your hand and guide you through uncertainty? While you may be unsure and unsteady, they stand confidently because of their vantage point, position, and track record. That was Bev for me. She was instrumental in the early success I enjoyed as diverse supplier and impacted my life in a meaningful way.

We initially met at J&J. At the time, I was a designer in IT while she was leading the global supplier diversity and inclusion practice. There, she stood as a trusted advocate for how small, women-owned and minority-owned businesses worked with J&J. The important thing to note is that while being a J&J leader who was focused on doing the right thing for the enterprise, Bev also acted as an interpreter—helping diverse suppliers navigate their seat at the table and benefit from all that the corporation had to offer. She did that with a lot of care and pride. When I took a leap and launched my design business, Bev insisted that I get certified as a Diverse Supplier. Once I did, I, too, enjoyed the benefits of her wisdom, care, and expertise as I negotiated the new landscape of working with J&J from the outside. She looked out for me in many important ways, so I feel a sense of loyalty to make sure that whatever she does that includes me, shines. I want to make her proud and pay forward all I've received from her. I'm a lucky part of her legacy.

It's so crucial to seek out sponsors like Bev, because often you're in spaces where you're the only one like you, or one of a few. Bev was the kind of leader in the room that would connect and care to know what you needed to be successful. Her willingness to make herself available to you blew me away. Prior to launching my business, I spent ten years at J&J and loved the company. With Bev's help, I was able to preserve a healthy relationship with a company I genuinely cared for, while nurturing the new one I was building. I know how rare and special an experience that was.

As we dare to do big things in the world, it helps to believe in something: a guiding motto, a set of principles, or values. Bev and I learned how J&J made all its decisions guided by a clear belief like this: The Credo. So when it came to designing a brand for SEE Company, we shared the same view of the significance of a brand that stands for something. A brand whose purpose was to see everyone elevated. As we crafted the logo, chose colors, fonts, and shaped the brand's visual language, every step was imbued with meaning (who the brand is, who it serves, why it exists, why people should believe).

The ethos that guides my design approach is to "articulate the meaningful". It's a joy to help purpose-driven leaders like Bev express their identity, ideas, and audacious dreams in the form of design that is true, beautiful, and enduring. We did with SEE Company. As it grows up, continuing to live up to its promise, I hope it endears in the hearts and minds of the people it serves. I hope it continues to make Bev proud as a key part of her legacy, born from purpose, for a purpose.

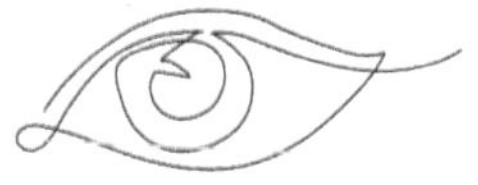

Chapter 5

Believe in Bonds

"You don't know what your abilities are until you make a full commitment to developing them."

—Carol S. Dweck,
EDUCATOR

HOLDING A BEAUTIFUL brand in my hand, it was time for serving people. Action is embedded in branding. What is your everyday walk? What moves life are decisions. Our decisions based off our choices and values.

Every day, we are our personal brand. We must remember this for every touchpoint. Then in the brand for your company, one would hope your personal values and what your personal brand stands for synergizes with your professional life and brand. With David's help, I determined what SEE is and what it isn't. As a leader, your personal brand comes through more than any company brand. That's why clarity around your values is essential. When I talked about life purpose, it speaks to what my personal brand is all about. When I moved into this new season from corporate life, where values were instilled through the credo, it was easy for me to challenge myself on when I built those values for SEE Company. How does that flow from me as an individual into the creation of SEE Company and the values around the company? In the end, it was almost a seamless flow because I understood myself when I built these values, who I am, what I stand for, and what I am at this time. I could have been born a century ago or a century ahead, but there's a reason I've been born in the season of this life. Some people believe that the soul lives on and on, over many lifetimes, and what you carry with you that's common in all those lifetimes is your soul.

I believe your soul evolves over time. I don't know if and when, before or after—all I can do is show up for this one and be clear on what I believe, what I stand for, and the why of my being here. I've found throughout my journey so far is when you can give love to everything you do, the work you choose, if love is at the center, it seems like everything else flows. I'm not saying everything is perfect. Sometimes it's harder to receive love when you're such a giver. As I age and grow, I feel it's more important to receive love more. It shows up in so many forms. You can't pinpoint, *oh, that's love!* You can pinpoint with people. My niece, Rayna, sent the nicest gift to me while traveling for a leadership program —she thought about me. A décor sign that says, "I love you to the beach and back." That is a gesture of love. It doesn't have to be something big. It can be a compliment, listening ear, or an offering of time.

Let's not be afraid to use the word, LOVE. And I try to use it more in my everyday lexicon. Giving love is important to me. I'm still learning how to receive love better. That's part of my journey I have to work on. People who know me feel that light of love that generally comes through me. I wouldn't know any other way to be. Enjoying life: people say take time to smell the roses. It's really the ability to live in the present and see it as joy. Enjoy. When you enjoy life, that also implies you are participating in it and looking for it. Sometimes we miss the joys in their simplest form—the sun, your pet's subtle actions. I really live in my values. When people talk about personal brand, they almost take it and compartmentalize it over here to the side. It's touching, seeing, sensing and feeling. It comes out in your daily walk. If you can find synergy in what you believe about your purpose and you can walk that, it becomes part of your personal brand. In other decisions around branding, if you can manifest that inward to outward, now you got it! SEE Company needed to emanate diversity, inclusivity, and sustainability. On trend, on time, on everyone's mind!

As Forbes contributor Ron Carucci states in his January 24, 2024, piece, "The data are unmistakably clear. Companies committed to diversity and inclusion significantly outperform those that aren't." Here, Carucci is breaking down the most poignant data from the December 2023 edition of the "McKinsey Diversity Matters" report aggregating info from 1,265 companies in 23 countries.

- 39 percent increased likelihood of outperformance for those in the top quartile of ethnic representation versus the bottom quartile

- Companies with representation of women exceeding 30 percent (and thus in the top quartile) are significantly more likely to financially outperform those with 30 percent or fewer

- Companies in the top quartile for ethnic diversity show an average 27 percent financial advantage over others

- Those in the bottom quartile for both (ethnic and gender diversity) are 66 percent less likely to outperform financially on average, up from 27 percent in 2020

From a brand standpoint—one that steps up and stands out for inclusion—I can tell you what these percentages illustrate: Higher rates of innovation, the lifeblood of a product or service. Creativity flows when you have a team of people from different backgrounds working together. Points of view will all be unique. Ideas form and flow into the next. Skillsets merge and transfer. The common goals elevate into an innovation that's both novel and useful. The ability to conceive, develop, deliver and scale together is then a process that is dynamic, not stagnant. You want that vibe to last. It feels magical as hidden treasures are revealed. Diversity can't be priced in or priced out. The material gleaned is simply more lustrous than the Hope Diamond!

I'm always looking for ways to enhance relationships I already have, and I look for innovative ways to expand my orbit. The most powerful capital is relationship capital. The more we can all use these relationships for the highest good, then we can really see everyone elevate. Concurrently, know that creative partnerships, all relationships, take time. If your time was once governed by ripping and running through corporate America, you may not have a developed sense of time yet, as crazy as that sounds.

Believe Your Time Is Precious

Retirement can be a bit of a grieving process even when you're exhilarated by the thoughts and plans of starting anew. Allow yourself this duality. How phenomenal that our heart can feel different emotions at one time, making use of the twenty-seven different emotions that you may possess. I experienced an identity shift. Anytime you are moving from one season to another, whether from a loss, retirement, job change, life puts you in this space where you really get to choose who you want to be and what you want to do. When you're in the corporate world, everything is framed. Now, this amazing freedom allows you to be who you are. It is the most freeing and enriching experience. To do it my way without having to explain to anyone. There are no rules, but I have experiences in my backpack to pull from. If we're talking about fashion, I put on my manufacturing hat. I was manufacturing contact lenses then and now it's clothes. I just saw a friend who said, "I don't know who I am or what I'm doing. You just jump right in!"

I advised, "First of all, don't compare yourself to others. Be you. Comparing does not serve anyone, but if you want to do a smart comparison, it would be an appreciation for where that person is in their journey. We all have journeys. Mine is unscripted."

Before leaving my corporate cocoon, I coached a few companies pro bono. It was testing ground for me also, a win-win. The innovation lab, so to speak, helped me make gain clarity and make decisions. I was able to identity what steps or issues seemed to take up the most time.

You can get pulled in a lot of directions. Believe me, when you open the retirement door, plenty of nonprofits, board opportunities, creative partners will knock and attempt to fill up your time. Before you answer, make yourself a cup of coffee, take in the aroma, feel the steam on your face, and think about how you want to spend your time. Don't go for the shiny and new right away. It may be fleeting and not align with your purpose. Sometimes it's not a hard no but a "let me think of someone else who can help" or "have you thought of this skill or class that may help you see another way". See and believe together over that cup of coffee! It doesn't have to be an extended commitment on your part. The universe tells you if it's right. Don't ignore that voice.

I know now that I'm here to give. Giving comes in a variety of forms. While conceiving my brand, within two years, I lost my mother, sister, and brother. They reminded me that life is precious and must be lived to the fullest rather than succumbing to grief. Protect your energy and the company and their energy you keep. If you feel like something is missing, it may be because *you* are missing. There is a balance between serving others and serving ourselves. Put yourself first. Love yourself through it all.

When I fell in love with someone other than myself for the first time, I was twenty-two years old. Going through that marriage for five years, I had to deal with getting through. He was clueless. I was clueless. We were too young. He ran wild.

When I reflect on this and think of how I spent my time, I realize that something moved beneath the surface. We never said goodbye. He didn't show up to the divorce hearing. Consequently, I never gained closure. Upon realizing this, I gave myself permission to say, "Goodbye."

The lesson is being aware of what you're going through before jumping straight to starting a company or taking another job. Process. There is always an obligation to someone else or a compromise or way to bend yourself to comply. Sometimes we do this to people-please, but there may be more at play under the surface that we're avoiding or not processing. If you, too, are in retirement, or reinventing, you must reframe in order to make the most of your time and energy.

"To reimagine, you need a full *review* of what's going on first. Know where you are," writes former *Vogue* and *Harper's Bazaar* editor Maureen Lippe in her book, *Radical Reinvention.* "Have the courage to reassess your life journey to discover how to transform your future from one of disappointment into an opportunity for progress. You must work on yourself with intention bringing a sense of meaning and purpose to your life. If that inner voice is poking at you, something is misaligned. Only you can identify what that is. Only you can realign. The sooner you are aware, the sooner you hit the road with your emotional belongings. These belongings may only be the mental material of a disruption."

Maureen adds that the review is about coming to terms with the full breadth of experience and emotions. I allowed myself to do this when I felt stuck on not having closure with my ex. It was legitimately taking up time and energy with soreness that I had not stopped to feel because of all the hours I worked.

She adds: "Without review, you float or wallow with no anchor, and you might find yourself in oblivion. You pay attention to nothing. If you don't perform a review, an assessment of what occurred, along with your current circumstances, the lack of concrete data in your heart and brain is dangerous, causing an explosion of consequences that may set you back twice as far as the actual event. Judgment is impaired. There is no clarity. Some decisions can't wait. It's all overwhelming filled with uncertainty, but you must ask yourself who you want to now be. The review is the beginning of the journey to survival; it is unpredictable and uncontrollable at first. It takes brave work." With my own closure out of the way, action came easier for SEE. There were no longer smudges on my lenses of possibilities.

On the services side, we realized I move comfortably between coaching, advising, consulting so kind of a hybrid. I wanted to work with diversity-forward companies, inclusion-focused corporations and people-centered investors on supplier diversity. I wanted to continue to help businesses. I started a few contracts, and I decided I would not work with competing suppliers. I didn't want to feel like this was "work" after working for forty years straight. I was looking to build a brand starting with what I knew. Then I wanted to expand from there.

For social media, I thought of the thousands of women business owners I had worked with. Many were strong relationships, like Doubletake, Terri Hall's marketing and PR agency. At the same time, I reached out to my dear friend, Michael Byron, who was senior director of supplier inclusion at Walmart, for a list of fashion designers because I wanted to get back into retail. Time to channel that young girl twirling around in her sister's clothes.

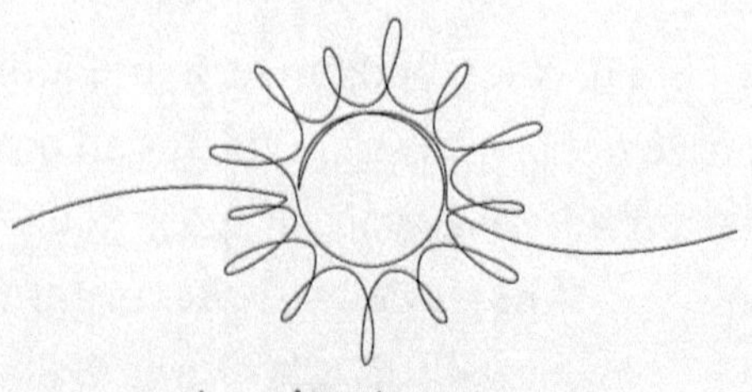

Light Lessons

Terri Hall On Staying Relevant

I met Bev years ago through WBENC. We served on the marketing committee. She was the chair and had received multiple awards during that time. I always admired her. When she started SEE, she talked to the executive VP of marketing at WBENC, an organization of over 17,000 women-owned businesses nationwide. It's divided into regional partner organizations. Florida, New York, South, fourteen partnerships. I'm the board chair of the regional partner in Florida. Bev asked the CEO of the regional partner for three names. I was one of them.

Don't ever forget the power of network. Your name will come up! Stay relevant.

I began my career working for a couple of boutique advertising agencies and after a couple of years, one of the clients (an electronics distribu-tion company) hired me as their marketing and PR person. That opportunity fl ourished to a point—until I fully understood my worth and knew it was time to move on.

I started my own agency with heavy graphic design and advertising, then morphed into PR. The client base changed. We created campaigns for zoos, attractions, the Florida aquarium in Tampa and beyond. Tech changed all this from drafting tables to desktops. I was commuting across the bridge every to Tampa every day for long meetings at the office. Then satellite office, two days a week. What changed everything was when my accountant told me I was spending 500 hours a year on the road! My commute stopped that week.

Whether you want to glide and soar with it or not, change occurs quickly in our digitally driven world.

I was always the youngest person in the room and now I'm not. You have to keep your thoughts young and always continue to learn. Have a wide range of people of different ages. Love what you do, love the people you work with, which will amp up your productivity and keep your mind sharp.

The hardest thing for staying the course with your brand is staying several years. It's your business. It's lonely at the top sometimes. I can remember calling my mom laying on the floor and crying that I didn't have enough business to survive. Listen to feedback. Create a system of checks and balances for yourself.

Bev is the brand. She truly wants to see

everyone elevate. The apparel and accessories are a byproduct of who she really is. If you have beliefs, align yourself with a larger group to learn from or collaborate with—that can make all the difference. To keep your mind in "elevate" mode, maintain your focus. Don't get distracted by noise.

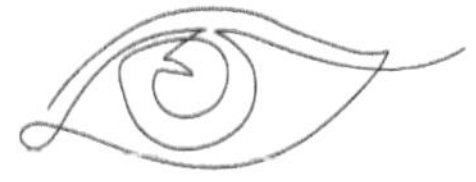

Chapter 6

Wearing Is Believing

"Exploration is the engine that drives innovation. Innovation drives economic growth. So, let's all go exploring."

—Edith Widder,
OCEANOGRAPHER AND MARINE BIOLOGIST

CLOTHING IS A special memory for me because of how it made me feel as a young girl, as a woman and as a professional executive. I returned to retail designing apparel. When it was time to pivot, I told myself to rewind and start with retail, business to consumer. I could have started anywhere, but I wanted to start with something you can see. You can't see service. It matters. You can see clothes, and clothes can change someone's perspective about you.

The initial designer I worked with had created apparel for Venus Williams, and I had once supervised an international manufacturing department of 1,200 people. This combination counted for a great deal. We worked together on apparel designs, went back and forth for a year. I wanted high-end sustainable fashions. I wanted to go end to end with diverse suppliers to walk the talk.

On a day that vibrated with so much good, we got through our first photo shoot. This highly skilled designer's daughter was our first model. We had completed two collections, as well as accessories. It took eighteen months to get through that cycle. Lessons learned? I had managed boys, girls, infants' departments at JC Penney, and knew that stitching, small accents, counted. I've been involved with every bit of the design for every single item. What surprised me was how much retail had changed. We're strictly eCommerce. How do you sell online and make your brand stand out when you don't have splendid displays and clothing racks to pull from, or mirrors to see the clothes on your shape?

When you hear it takes three to five years before you turn a profit on an apparel business, that's true unless you get a celebrity endorser. If you do, your supply chain better be ready. I've also committed to the US and diverse businesses. I was disappointed with the level of handholding necessary for the different suppliers. We were relying on suppliers to help on sourcing and delivery. Fortunately, I had done planning, sourcing with J&J, JCP, Sara Lee. It didn't feel foreign, but I felt dated. It's different when it's your money and you're making finite details on something that may not sell.

I had always wanted my brand to reflect being able to offer services or products. I knew it would be something endearing across products and for designs in the future. One of our spectacular designers in London, Patrick Morrison of Furious Goose, or "exuberant British accessories", nailed our signature design with many options into many forays. When I look at it, I think about the values and how these were interwoven into the thought process around that design. When Patrick approached this, I asked him to keep our Believe values in mind. Let's be sure we *inspire, innovate, enhance well-being.* It needs to be part of our everyday conversation, in the value chain, from design to delivery. That's when a brand comes to life. It's not simply words in a poster on the wall. Your brand is part of how you maneuver in your business for every decision, every action, to drive results. All the better if that navigation tool can be adorned with a symbol, logo, signature design or color that displays your brand. Today, mine is the Reversible Tunic because feeling is believing!

Inspire and Innovate

What do great teams do? Form, storm, norm, perform. The *inspire and innovate* value of SEE Company is a catalyst. I base all on the energy I'm feeling. Thus, with services of the brand, I have purposefully decided to only take on certain clients because I want to devote equal time for services and products. I'm consulting on their growth strategies. I realize that I have to be patient because it can be a long journey from recommending a client to onboarding. I want to have positive messaging for everybody and use my time for these touchpoints that are personal, heartfelt and deep.

I'm not competing with anyone else. I'm doing what I believe in and building a brand for the long term to leave a legacy. I was just talking to a startup that one of my clients wanted me to coach and guide. This woman was all over the place, so I knew I could point out two or three things that could make her life a little better and help her sleep more. I could see that on her face, it went from her letting me know all she knew, which was great, to the weight of a new business, trying to pitch it the right way, trying to make her value proposition clear. In that hour, I know it made a difference in her life. I tried to inspire her to innovate.

In another call with someone, she said, "Sales are down, and I hired all these people." I could almost feel the phone sagging. She felt really low from that weight of the business.

I beamed, "I noticed on the website you did this, that, and a year ago, it was that." She was thrilled that someone noticed. So, the next step for me to keep her energy up was say, "So, now, let's talk about how you can build on that progress!" At the Billion Dollar Roundtable conference recently, Director of Global Economic Inclusion and Business Diversity at Merck Raul Suarez-Rodriguez and I were heading to a celebratory dinner.

He said, "Life is something. Do you remember you were recruiting me for supplier diversity? I really thought about it. I would have loved to work with you." But at that time, he had another offer.

I said, "And look at you now!" His face absolutely glowed. People remember how you made them feel. When you can see that difference, it's priceless. I can remember another situation in Orlando at a conference. I try to tune in if I get intuition. I had walked past someone, and my gut urged, "Go back." I had gone past registration and this little voice said, "Turn around and go back." I grumbled and said to myself, *why?* You do get these little signals. I went back and this woman came from the side running up to me. She wasted no time in communicating her distress. "I was hoping I would see you! I'm less than an hour from meeting with my team, and I was going to announce that we're closing the business. People will lose jobs." The tears flowed. "I've been dealing with this, and it's just so hard!"

I said, "Dry your eyes, and let's find a conference room to talk this through before you go in to meet with your group."

I asked for a quick synopsis. They had lost two or three clients for whatever reason it was. I said, "Let's revisit why you started this business in the first place. Tell your team you want to delay the meeting for later this afternoon, and let's walk through this."

I took her on a journey based on the customer journey map. She had been in corporate America and wanted to do her own thing. "Along the way, were there any times where you had to meet the moment?" I inquired.

Her response filled me in on the past five loaded years. Her body language started to shift. She perked up, welcoming this opportunity to contemplate her journey and reflect. Her eyes sparkled while forgetting the current crisis and telling me the story of her business. I said, "You will meet some future moments." Her sigh was so gigantic it was like she was breathing in the strength of the whole universe.

You can create a shift in moments of distress that can literally change your life and the lives of others. Then we talked about her role as the leader besides founding this company and calling herself CEO.

"What it comes down to is love," I said. "Do you love this business?"

She said, "I do, but there are times I hate it too."

"Well, what leader doesn't have these moments? We do this in relationships. Are you okay delaying closing up the business?"

She shook her head. "I am for now."

"So, how can we change the conversation you will have with your team? Let's create a turnaround." She wrote some ideas down on her little pad. Current state and future state. The middle counts. This is where the action is—instigated, executed by your people. What three actions over three to six months could turn this around?

She did keep her business open for another several months because she believed something new. If we understood the power of belief, it would make all the difference.

A company out of New York City had a similar situation. I received an early Saturday morning call from someone drowning in tears. "And who is this please?" She was in a financial hole and needed investors. I said, "It's like a child. You're turning your back on your child."

We had met months before on this particular stage that needed the most nurturance. She abandoned the child, expecting it to grow on its own. Now, she was pulling money out of her core business to feed this new business. She had issues with the current partners. It was emotional upheaval, not business upheaval. You see, I had coached her three times prior to this Saturday call on the same themes, and she had not taken the advice. She was very impulsive.

Nevertheless, I made a call to the CPO to mentor her company and they later became a new supplier, and millions later, they are thriving.

Learning Is Elevating

People asked me why I was rolling out clothing under my brand, as if I had to be one-dimensional. I'm multifaceted. And I guess you could say the fabric for SEE Company was sewn early on in my life.

One of my favorite things to do as a girl was enter beauty pageants. I would wait until a couple of days before the event to tell my mother (so it would be too late to back out). I don't remember winning any, but I got accolades, and a few years later, homecoming queen. But it was more about having a new outfit and enjoying competing and being on stage. The pageantry centered on how it made me feel because it was quite a confidence builder.

In the eighth grade, when I got to make my first dress in a home economics class, it was a V-neck dress that had a special meaning to me because my mom only had three dresses at the time. I knew my mom always wanted more dresses but sacrificed for us kids so we could have more clothes. Over time, my mom slowly expanded her wardrobe and I got to watch her confidence grow and learned how clothing became her language of love for herself and her kids.

One of the happiest days in her life was on her seventy-fifth birthday. I surprised Mom with her first shopping spree, a $1,000 Dillard's gift card shopping spree presented by the department manager. I told her to go to Dillard's because she had an appointment there at 10:00 a.m. The store was in Dothan, Alabama, less than an hour from her home. I coordinated with the manager who treated my mom like a special guest. What a day! She selected several outfits to wear to church and other occasions. When she got home, she called me with tears of joy. I will always remember her screeching with glee, "They treated me like a celebrity". They say clothes does not make the man, but clothes elevated my mom.

Another experience occurred when my older sister bought me a special outfit from the extra money she had earned from a summer job. I had just entered my early teens and was starting to show curves, so she decided to get me a black popcorn bodysuit with cream-colored, hip hugger pants and a pair of chunky heel shoes to go with it. When I put it on and looked at myself in the mirror, it was my first realization I was transitioning from a girl to a woman. It was this beautiful awareness about how clothes can make a person feel. I observed how it gave a person confidence in my mom and felt the difference it could make on how a person sees themselves as I did when I wore that outfit.

Those experiences stayed with me when I went to college as I thought about what career I might pursue. During my senior year, as I walked across campus, I greeted the dean of students who was talking with Mickey Farley, a business executive visiting the campus that day. The dean asked me what I was looking to do upon graduation, and I replied that I was looking at retail because of my interest in business and clothes, as well as my desire to work with customers.

Mickey said, "It just so happens I'm in retail," as he was responsible for HR at his company on a regional level. He said enthusiastically, "With your smile and how friendly you are, we should have a conversation about you working at our company!"

At the time I was one of only a few Black women at my college. The executive, Mickey, and the entire regional management staff at Mickey's company were white. And when I started working at this company, I was the only African American woman on the management team at that store. Attending an all-Black school until I was fourteen, I knew opportunities like this did not come along often. I realized at that moment that Mickey was giving me a proverbial seat at the table in business and opening a door that was otherwise closed. I had been seen and recognized for my potential as a leader.

I don't mind sharing all sides of me. It makes life more interesting when you're able to move comfortably from parts of your life. I was involved in so many different companies and had to shift so often. Let's talk about *this, that,* connect you to this person.

I listen to subject matter experts and try to not stifle their creativity. I tend to be a decisive leader, and I like progress. Still, being decisive and striving to win doesn't mean there aren't setbacks—especially in the early stages, which I'm sure all business owners can relate to.

When a supplier we contracted didn't help us on the

packaging as contracted, we had to source and make do with the requirements. She could have shortened that cycle time for us. We could have avoided mistakes like redoing labeling. Something as simple as the privacy policy on eCommerce business I've learned. Every day we're learning new things. Another disappointment was on the run time of trademarking, which is somewhat mind-numbing. After all, while you're waiting, your brand is unprotected.

The gains, the look of success, makes the growing pains worth it.

The decision to start is always the hardest decision. As I embark on every new SKU, it's a decision to start. Every time we add an accessory, the tie, pocket square and socks in the men's line, it drives me. SEE is the kind of brand that moves in different categories. The sky is the limit. Every time we release a new product, we bring in a new model to propel as an ambassador.

Two years ago, we launched in Tampa with a fashion show during Women's History Month. Last year, we did photoshoots with former Miss America Ericka Dunlap, who is SEE brand ambassador. Having met decades before, we reconnected at Girl Friends Conclave in Mexico. It was a new opportunity to collaborate. And we are sorors of Delta Sigma Theta! Some consider her a sight for sore eyes. I would like to think the clothes Ericka's wearing elevate and sprinkle a little magic on her personal brand also.

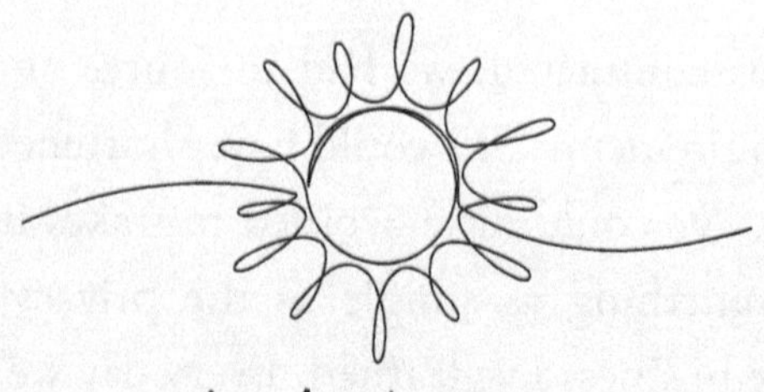

Light Lessons

Ericka Dunlap On Elevating Courage

Bev and I met in passing, but within a few moments, she extended a graciously warm validation and seal of approval, which meant the world to me. She was minutes away from delivering a keynote address for a packed audience at the annual NMSDC conference and people were clamoring all around her. The gentleman who introduced us encouraged her to exchange information and mentor me because I was a Miss America who championed Diversity and Inclusion. With that, Bev immediately said, "She looks like a Black Barbie!", to which point I chuckled at the idea of this giant in the corporate landscape giving me that type of commendation.

You see, from my perspective, the beauty queen is forever merited by her appearance, and she is particularly scrutinized by other women. From younger women who measure your validity and relevance based on age shaming and from older women who expect you to be a dingbat without a mind of your own, scruples, capabilities, and competence until you prove yourself worthy.

That was my ordinary experience. One of Maya Angelou's most famous quotes is, "You may forget what people said to you, but you will never forget how they make you feel."

In a matter of seconds, Bev Jennings made me feel seen, and regardless of how big of a presence she had in the corporate world, she recognized that I had some kind of talent that she could connect to and possibly hone. She gave me her number and the seed of our friendship was planted.

At the time, I was in the midst of a career shift and aligning with someone like Bev was an answered prayer. Because my platform for Miss America was cultural diversity and inclusion, I was deeply tapped into that world from the lens of workforce diversity. Supplier diversity, on the other hand, required a more finely tuned skillset, and I was adjusting to the new environment. Not only did Bev carve time to reach out and return calls, but she also endorsed connections and sponsored conversations on my behalf, like she would a niece or a favored past intern. She courageously advocated for me and encouraged me toward pursuing my professional goals. Her delivery was always clear and kind-hearted, a unique dichotomy in the corporate culture.

She shared insights for growth and opportunities for development—again, foreign concepts in the beauty pageant industry; especially for a little Black girl from the South. Little did I know, Bev, too, was a Florida native, from a small town with big dreams.

I am a third-generation Floridian, from Orlando. My childhood was effortless, full of love and ambition, so much so, that I retired from my first career by age twenty-two when I won the coveted title of Miss America 2004 after fifteen years of pageant competitions.

Pageantry is a Southern tradition and denotes the qualities of a Southern Belle or Debutante. When I was three, my sister, eighteen years older, was a fashion design major in college, and I was her mini model. As the muse for her final project for the 1984 spring semester, she carefully coordinated an entire fashion show from concept, patterns, designs, media, and production. I was her finale surprise, donning something very 80s inspired and similar to one of the adult models. As I sashayed the runway, I recall the audience laughing, whistling, and cheering me on, and I loved every minute of it!

Fashion shows were all the rage at that time in history with the staunch shoulder pads, bodacious ruffles, and big, fluffy everything. Imagine this tiny person with these oversized clothes. It was adorable, special, and hilarious. While I was lovingly utilized as her gimmick, the experience was the catalyst to me being comfortable on stage and learning how to effectively communicate the story of the garment and the narrative of the designer at a young age.

When I was six, my mom brought me a brochure for a pageant, and I immediately saw stars. I was ready for the stage, but Mom and I had no idea what to do, how to get started or how to make the investment worthwhile. One of my neighbors was a master seamstress who was known for her skillful technique in creating bountiful ruffles with organza and fishing wire. This required a special sewing machine, which not many people would have. My mom convinced my dad that the $600 for the dress was a deal considering the time it would take to create the masterpiece. Of course, my dad had sticker shock for weeks on end, but after winning the second pageant, it all made sense and we were hooked! That day, in the middle of the Osceola Square Mall, you could have told me I was Miss America right then and there, and I would've believed it! I was ecstatic, my mom was overjoyed, and my dad felt vindicated for the cost of the dress.

In those days, the girls who consistently won those children pageants were textbook gorgeous blondes with button noses, or adorable brunettes with perfectly coifed hairstyles and expensive, coordinating attire. There were not a lot of girls of color who competed, and I was generally the only one in most competitions. During any random weekend, one competition could easily range between $500-$1500. There were the competition fees, lodging and travel and of course, the outfits and accessories for all of the different categories. It was a high-stakes game, a gamble if you will. A successful weekend meant that you won at minimum a portion of the investment back. But there were no guarantees. Each competition yielded a different outcome with different contestants and different judges.

Very early on, I learned the valuable assets of confidence and courage. Because I knew I was different looking from the status quo, I knew that I had to bolster the confidence to blow them away in an interview. I knew that I had to come up with a complete answer that resonated with something that was true to my heart and my vast six-year-old imagination. In that mall pageant, another girl was asked where she wanted to go on vacation and she bashfully replied, "I don't know…Disneyworld?" And I thought, no, honey, you want to go to Paris! So, when it was my turn to answer that same question, that is precisely what I said, "I want to go to Paris because I want to see the Eiffel Tower."

In that moment, the judges nodded and smiled

with approval, and I knew I had impressed them. I learned how to establish my brand and communicate that brand identity that very day. Beyond the stage, I also sharpened the important skills of business development from the perspective of securing sponsorships, program book advertisements and communicating my brand, brand promise and vision.

One of the key takeaways from my time in working with Bev over the years is her commitment to the process of building a brand. She believes that when you're in alignment and operating in integrity, great things naturally come together and oftentimes, all you have to do is show up.

One of my personal mantras is, "No matter how you feel—Get up! Dress up! Show up! And NEVER give up!" Get up each day and dress like the professional you aspire to be. If you elect not to get up and get going, you merely procrastinate your purpose. Make sure you're not fumbling that opportunity to have another day to advance, to do something to make yourself better. I am constantly evolving and working on myself, for myself and for my precious daughter, and it is due in large part to luminaries like Bev Jennings, who are able to see and believe the good in everyone who puts forth a solid effort. I hope that one day, my sweet girl sees Mommy's effort, embraces my mentorship, and harnesses an unstoppable energy and inner light that can be used to navigate the world and manifest the life that she deserves. All in all, I sincerely hope that I am paying it forward for my daughter and other future leaders to see and believe as Bev Jennings did for me.

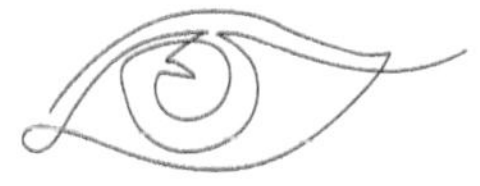

Chapter 7

Feel, Speak and Live Your Values

"The world needs many more dreamers. Unreasonable souls who fight the urge to be ordinary."

—ROBIN S. SHARMA,
LEADERSHIP EXPERT

SEE COMPANY IS comprised of over 80% of our employees, suppliers and contractors are women, minority and/or LBGT. On top of that, every material we use to create our hand-crafted accessories and clothing is carefully selected from sustainable materials.

In being at the forefront of diversity and inclusion, there are outside forces that counter what we see and stand for. It's been eye-opening for me. There are assaults on diversity. A prominent policymaker wants to fight with Mickey

Mouse, symbolic of an iconic brand that has endured for a century in bringing creativity, joy, and possibility to billions of people through the generations.

Last year, Florida's governor signed legislation that banned public colleges from using tax dollars to implement or promote DEI initiatives. The Florida board of education followed suit, defining DEI as "programs that categorize individuals based on race or sex for the purpose of differential or preferential treatment". The education board also said that a "principles of sociology" course could no longer be taught and would be replaced with a general American history class. closing its office of the chief diversity officer, eliminating DEI positions and administrative appointments, and halting DEI-focused contracts with outside vendors.

There are so many factors that influence political decisions. Most people want to do good. What ends up happening is they get caught up in expectations of others and they want to belong. They want to hold the jobs. There is such a high desire to belong, and social media can destroy or propel. They are dealing with things we didn't have to deal with twenty years ago. Behind all the rhetoric and vitriol, it's based in fear. If people understood this, we would understand politicians more. They have families too. They don't want their lives threatened. They don't want to lose what they have. Then you have some that are just seeking and eager to use power. Some have always been that way. That one vote is my voice. Use your voice to contrast dark and light.

At the time of the assaults, Disney was making "Wish", an animated musical-comedy welcoming audiences to the magical kingdom of Rosas, where Asha, an Afro-Hispanic, sharp-witted idealist, makes a wish so powerful that it is answered by a cosmic force—a little ball of boundless energy called Star. Together, Asha and Star confront a most formidable foe—the ruler of Rosas, King Magnifico—to save her community and prove that when the will of one courageous human connects with the magic of the stars, wondrous things can happen.

There will always be the battle between light and darkness. Stay the course emitting your own values—even when the raindrops of discord and disconnect are falling around you.

Sometimes you must see the numbers to believe the story of impact. As detailed in the "Beyond Supplier Diversity to Economic Empowerment: BDR 2023 Report", which was sponsored by Cummins and JPMorgan Chase & Co, Billion Dollar Roundtable members spent a combined $122,728,416,593 with suppliers and contractors that fall within the BDR's diversity categories. This spend led to an estimated economic impact of $320.545 billion. The spend also supported an estimated 1,763,546 jobs, resulted in an estimated $93.05 billion in wages paid, and an estimated $171.17 billion of value added (business profits and taxes).

The totality of this economic empowerment cannot be understated in terms of the actual supply chain dollars that go to suppliers. In addition, there is measurement of economic activity stemming from spend via jobs, tax revenue and other benefits produced that boosts communities where corporations and diverse suppliers do business, on top of the training, engagement, technical assistance, business mentorships, and network the BDR provides. I am one of the BDR advisors.

In the stories of inclusivity being created here, the light is as luminous as the brightest laser beam (which is even brighter than the sun. My light is bringing on suppliers to build the brand, create jobs even if a few, and have that voice and let everyone know our brand is very much a brand for diversity, inclusivity and sustainability. That al eady stands for something and opposes views.

Michelle Obama said, "When they go low, we go high."

Empathy Elevates Everyone

I went back to my Johnson & Johnson home for our $2 billion supplier spend celebration. A friend and I, both having retired, were dressed almost alike. Someone said, "We can tell you're both no longer in corporate America. You're wearing open-toe shoes!"

People have embraced working virtually because it

brings them closer to being themselves. There is no substitute for self. What we see is what we believe. You must look beyond what you see and believe. When you talk culture, you're literally in it. We try to make culture group, but it's individual experience that sometimes happens in group experiences. In this whole era of belonging, I remember our chief diversity officer proposing this as her one big idea when it came to how she showed up for work and fulfilled this important role: "I feel myself." When you can feel yourself in any setting where you don't have to try to fit in, where you get to show as you, and you feel respected, heard, appreciated, there is so much power in just being who you are. Most people can't just be who they are. They're either on stage as in the world as it "is" and they will have to fit in the norms of corporate. When someone is different than the norm, they work hard to fit in to belong. When they go home, then they are who they are. There must come a time when everyone can be who they are. You still have emotional intelligence while navigating work protocol but not where it changes you from being you.

I smiled when I heard "I feel myself". I was a Credit Union board director in my early forties. We hired a young, smart, ambitious CEO, an Asian male. We used to talk about the importance of diversity and inclusion. He said their new mantra is, "Be yourself." It hit home so hard. It's so simple, but genius. When you can be yourself, it is the essence of culture. It's one of the hardest things to do because we're always so concerned with how people see us and judge us.

"Being an influential voice in diversity and inclusion requires more than just words; it demands empathy, the ability to thrive in diversity, and the willingness to feel and speak your beliefs," says Paul E. Wolfe, human first leadership advocate and author of *Human Beings First: Practices for Empathetic, Expressive Leadership.* "Each of us possesses the power to create change by embracing empathy, understanding the experiences of others, and advocating for inclusivity. We must recognize the importance of diverse voices and actively amplify them. By fostering an environment where everyone feels heard and valued, we can build a world where diversity flourishes, and equality becomes the norm."

With that in mind, for the onset of 2024, *Time* magazine asked experts to cite top mental health resolutions. Guy Winch, a clinical psychologist, author of *Emotional First Aid*, and co-host of the *Dear Therapists podcast*, stated, "Develop empathy for someone different from you" as No. 3. "Connect with someone from a group you have a moderate level of difficulty understanding. You could follow someone from a different political, religious, or ethnic background on social media, spend time in their community, or even read about a fictional character from that group. Aim to understand their perspective and read their emotions," he says. Try to be able to thoughtfully answer these questions: What makes this person happy? What makes them worried? What are their dreams? What experiences and emotions have shaped their world view? And how are their thought patterns similar to mine?"

As Fitch points out, people with high levels of empathy tend to function better in society than those with low levels—with more robust social networks and closer relationships.

Diversity is more about how every team member feels as authentic self than checking the box of a certain appearance that ultimately shows group variance. Diversity is more about feeling. Every individual wants to feel unique in tandem with being respected. This is elevation. I've watched people when they've been down and then elevate when you point out great things about them. The transformation flickers in their eyes. A family member and I were talking about body types, and she was feeling down about her curvaceous figure. I said, "Think of what some women pay for fake buttocks. You have something all these women are paying for!" She laughed. I could feel her energy shift in our conversation.

Sometimes all it takes is a little bit of empathy and change of language to make people feel lifted, appreciated, elevated. It takes so little to positively influence someone.

Global Head of Diversity, Equity of Inclusion for Louis Vuitton Moët Hennessey (LVMH) Greg Morley explains, "Understanding what your objective is the most important starting point in being influential. Once you have that objective in mind, preparation is important, learning the context of the situation in which you are entering and endeavoring to influence and helping others see beyond the obvious is our role as advocates and professionals. Remember that what may seem very basic and obvious to you, could be complex, intimidating, even scary to a non-practitioner. I was reminded of this recently when speaking with the head of the high school I attended. A smart, progressive, and empathetic man, he was trying to understand the perspective of different stakeholders relating to diversity and inclusion and it was not a topic in which he was either an expert or where he had time to become one. He genuinely wants to make a positive difference in the lives of those associated with the school community, giving these diverse members a strong sense of inclusion and belonging. I believe our discussion helped him to untangle what was in front of him by understanding the needs and expectations of his various stakeholders and make sense of how he could achieve the aims of the school and the aspirations of students, teachers, staff and alumni."

With leaders like Paul E. Wolfe and Greg Morley, this world is a more empathetic place. People are being taken care of. Is planet? This is the new (and urgent era) of empathy that must be amped up. Earth is our mother who we need to care for.

Enrich Well-Being

In this value, SEE Company exemplifies respect for the environment, how things are disposed of, and the sourcing of organic fabrics. More specifically, every yard of fabric has a sustainable label on the products. Even in making of buckle and medallion, stainless steel is more sustainable. Where possible, where we can, we use recyclable packing, working with partners that foster goals around sustainability.

The "McKinsey Diversity Matters" report cited herein not only measured the financial growth of 330 companies they had been tracking eight years of representative data—it surveyed holistic impact. In other words, prioritization of social and environmental goals.

The authors summarize, "In many parts of the world there is a growing call for organizations to consider their holistic impact, not only within their own business environment, but on a wider scale, both locally and globally. Our research points to five main areas of holistic impact: financial and operational, capabilities, health and workforce, and environmental and social. In this report, we broaden the lens of our research, placing particular focus on environmental and social-impact elements. Our findings are striking. Across all industries surveyed, more diversity in boards and executive teams is correlated to higher social and environmental impact scores."

With SEE's clarity on sustainability, I'm thrilled to hear of this momentum.

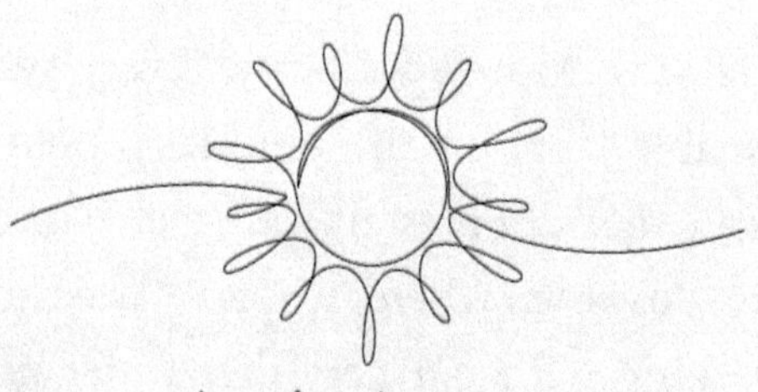

Light Lessons

Patricia Hill On Elevating Clarity

We've been programmed to be smart, get a PhD, stay in our head. However, we need creativity and heart to see and believe, and exercise emotional resonance.

When your learned imprints are on autopilot, you choose the old pattern and think you're choosing differently because you "know" it's wrong perhaps with age, but you're not. Once you know what your learned imprint is and what your trigger is, you pause and actually feel this is not the way to go here.

Back off. Calm down. Refocus. Come from a different perspective. Even when you know yourself, until you do that deeper work, you keep running off that old program.

Once you break the glitch, it only takes one time not to fall in the black hole. Step back. Let things be right now. You don't need to take action. Feel like you are in your true essence. In that essence, you will get clarity.

Listen outside of your box. Once you have made an agreement with yourself to transform, see differently and live differently.

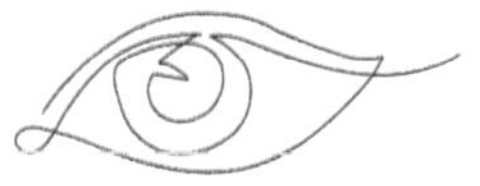

Chapter 8

See Everyone Elevate™

"When I look into the future, it's so bright it burns my eyes."

—OPRAH WINFREY,
HOST AND TELEVISION PRODUCER

THE "B" IN DEI has been absent from the lexicon, but it's the beating heart in the very anatomy of inclusion. Medriva reporter Anthony Raphael's definition of belonging is what I see and believe: "Cultivating an atmosphere where each person feels **recognized**, **valued**, and **understood**. This involves acknowledging the **unique contributions** and **potential** of every team member, while also providing them with the **safety** and **freedom** to **express** their **individuality**."

Being the visual person I am, I purposely boldfaced the muscle terms in this definition. They describe the vibrancy and frequency of belonging. If you have ever experienced exclusion, you feel the drastic difference.

"The challenge, however, lies in navigating generational norms and biases that can inadvertently hinder the realization of this ideal. Yet, through disciplined leadership practices, fostering a sense of belonging is not just possible; it's transformative."

A few of the practices Raphael recommends are avoiding favoritism, recognizing unique circumstances, and transitioning from a directive to a coaching style.

Paul E. Wolfe adds, "The world would be a place of boundless potential and collective growth if everyone felt seen. When we acknowledge and celebrate everyone's unique contributions and perspectives, we unlock a wellspring of innovation, creativity, and harmony. By lifting others up, we rise together, creating a society where every person can thrive and reach their fullest potential. Let us strive to see and elevate everyone, for in doing so, we pave the way for a more inclusive and prosperous future for all."

I know firsthand that coaching can be the difference between a business that shuts its doors and one that stays open! Some brands have folded because the founders did not see their true magnificence or feel that they were seen in a way that would help them elevate.

Greg Morley adds: "Our organisation recently conducted a global employee satisfaction survey, which gave individuals around the world the opportunity to have their say on a number of issues. The generally very positive feedback relating to the organisation being seen as diverse, inclusive and a place of safety and well-being were a cause of some celebration. With scores that were benchmarked against the best in class externally at 80 percent satisfied or highly satisfied, my thoughts went to 'the other 20 percent'. What had we missed? Where were they and how could we reach them? Follow-up feedback sessions have discovered that communications remains the biggest gap. In order to be seen, we need to focus on every employee knowing they are seen, heard and have safe avenues to share ideas, feedback and concerns. We hope to use the voices of some of these newly 'found' employees to elevate those of others who remain in the shadows."

How powerful! Another example of the depth and freedom of belonging and the need to find, see and elevating the remaining 20 percent.

How do I want SEE Company to elevate? The practical: By 2030, be highly profitable on the products side while making a significant economic impact. We may put some products on the radar we don't have today beyond clothing. There could be a tech play. Grow the accessories side. Support the nonprofit organizations. The SEE brand will be recognized in the global marketplace and when consumers purchase, I want them to know and be proud they're contributing to something bigger than themselves.

A brand never arrives. One would argue celebrity brands arrived and command the red carpet every time. However, every season, they elevate and present another dazzling face.

In times of uncertainty, I'm compelled to remember a flight with a stranger sitting next to me who was a new mom going on her first business trip since her daughter was born, in tears for most of the flight and feeling separated. She told me her story and I said, "It's not about perfection, it's about moving in a positive direction."

She stopped crying, smiled, and asked, "Who said that?"

I replied, "I did."

Look for opportunities to see everyone elevate!

Bev Jennings, CEO of SEE Company, founded SEE services offering to enable diversity-forward and inclusion-focused enterprises and people centered investors to achieve significant growth. As former Head of Global Supplier Diversity & Inclusion at Johnson & Johnson, she brings her C-level business knowledge, values-driven leadership and supplier diversity expertise to corporations and business owners, preparing them to succeed in an ever-changing environment.

With her signature approach and energy, Bev is leading SEE Company with her vision to "see everyone elevate". As a trusted advisor and certified business coach, she offers strategies and guidance for executives to deliver measurable success. Her three decades of executive experience span customer service, process excellence, end-to-end supply chain management and business development.

Bev also extends her knowledge to boards of growth-oriented organizations. She is an advisor to the Billion Dollar Roundtable (BDR), a non-profit of over 40 corporations spending $1 billion or more annually with diverse suppliers, which J&J joined as the first healthcare company. She is a member of the Board of Directors for Turtle, one of the largest independent electrical and industrial distributors and integrated supply services in the nation. Bev has served on several nonprofit boards.

She has been inducted into the WBE Hall of Fame, received WBENC Applause Award, Top 25 Leading Women Entrepreneur in New Jersey. the United Negro College Fund Masked Award, and Gateway Girl Scouts Woman of Distinction.

Bev holds an MBA in Industrial Management from the University of Dallas, is a Certified Master Business Coach from Fowler School of Business, and a BS degree in Management from the University of West Florida.

See and Believe is her debut book.

For more information, visit
http://seecompany.co.

References

Interviews

Doris Dickens. Phone. October 3, 2023.

Ericka Dunlap. In person. August 10, 2023.

Terri Hall. In person. August 10, 2023.

Patricia Hill. Phone. September 29, 2023.

Greg Morley. Written. February 7, 2024.

Necole Neal. Zoom. September 8, 2023.

David Ogunrinde. Zoom. September 5, 2023.

Paul E. Wolfe. Written. January 30, 2024.

Publications

Billion Dollar Roundtable. *Beyond Supplier Diversity to Economic Empowerment: BDR Report 2023.*

Carucci, Ron. "One More Time: Why Diversity Leads to Better Team Performance." *Forbes.* January 24, 2024. *https://www.forbes.com/sites/roncarucci/2024/01/24/ one-more-time-why-diversity-leads-to-better-team- performance/?sh=258e54277c74.*

Dixon-Fyle, Sundiatu, Celia Huber, María del Mar Martínez Márquez, Sara Prince, and Ashley Thomas. "Diversity matters even more: The case for holistic impact." McKinsey & Company. December 5, 2023. *https://www.mckinsey.com/*

featured-insights/diversity-and-inclusion/
diversity-matters-even-more-the-case-for-holistic-impact.

Editors of Encyclopedia Britannica. "Helen Keller." *Encyclopedia Britannica.*
https://www.britannica.com/biography/Helen-Keller.

Hall, Aaron. "The Power of Belief in Achieving Goals." *Insights.* August 26, 2023.
https://aaronhall.com/insights/the-power-of-belief-in-achieving-goals/#:~:text=Building%20confidence%20through%20belief%20is,yourself%20beyond%20your%20comfort%20zone.

Haupt, Angela. "9 Mental-Health Resolutions for 2024, According to Therapists." *Time.* December 27, 2023.
https://time.com/6371479/mental-health-resolutions-2024/.

Helmore, Edward. "University of Florida terminating all diversity, equity and inclusion positions." *The Guardian.* March 2, 2024.
https://www.theguardian.com/us-news/2024/mar/02/university-florida-diversity-equity-inclusion-positions.

IrisEyris, and Nicole Pivirotto. *Color, Form, and Magic.* Brooklyn, New York: IrisEyris, 2018.

Leider, Richard, and David Shapiro. *Who Do You Want to Be When You Grow Old?* Oakland, California: Berrett-Koehler, 2021.

Lenstore. "The significance of eyes around the world." *Lenstore Hub.*
https://www.lenstore.co.uk/eyecare/eyes-egypt-beyond-tale-eyes-different-cultures.

Lindner, Jannik. "The Most Surprising Diversity and Inclusion Statistics in 2024." Gitnux Market Data. December 20, 2023.
https://gitnux.org/diversity-and-inclusion-statistics/.

Lippe, Maureen. *Radical Reinvention.* New York, New York: Blue Moon Press, 2023.

Markel, Howard. "How Monet's artistic vision shone through
    ailing eyes." *PBS News Hour.* November 18, 2022.
    https://www.pbs.org/newshour/arts/
    how-monets-artistic-vision-shone-through-blurry-eyes.

Markson, Mitch. *The Imagination Playbook: For People, Brands,
    Issues, and Organizations.* New York, New York: Markson
    Ideacraft. February 2020.

Nerburn, Kent. *Simple Truths.* Novato, California: New World
    Library. 1996.

Raphael, Anthony. "Belonging: The New Frontier in Workplace
    Culture."

Medriva. March 3, 2024.
    https://medriva.com/business/
    belonging-the-new-frontier-in-workplace-culture.

SEE Company.
    https://seecompany.co/.

Wolfe, Paul E. *Human Beings First: Practices for Empathetic,
    Expressive Leadership.* Hartford, Connecticut: Publish Your
    Purpose. March 8, 2023.

9 798990 222328